This Time You Save Yourself

THIS TIME YOU
SAVE YOURSELF

BY ZARA BAS

This Time You Save Yourself by Zara Bas

ISBN: 9780645545586

Illustrated by PinnochiJo

Published by Zara Bas

www.goodthingsarewaiting.com

for tender hearts

contents

Breaking

This Time You Save Yourself

I know you're tired. I understand what you carry weighs you down and sometimes you feel like you're stuck in the quicksand you were so frightened of as a child. Or that you and your sadness are opposite poles of the world's strongest magnet.

But you must continue. Whether you believe it or not, there are times ahead that will bring you so much joy your body won't know what to do with it all. You will be moved to tears, to dance, to open arms and impulsive embraces. You will fall in love again with moments big and small - a friends laughter, purple tongue stains in the summer after handfuls of berries and falling asleep to the sound of the rain on tin rooftops.

You will celebrate and give thanks and fall to your knees, but this time it will be a result of overwhelming happiness instead of agony.

This Time You Save Yourself

You only have to look
at the state of my heart to see
that I never stopped choosing love

This Time You Save Yourself

You switch between shoes unfilled

nurturing mother
to protective father
supportive brother
and reliable sister
partner-in-crime best friend
and even-tempered teacher

you try to shield them
from harsh fantasies
and harsher realities
and while you play the part
mending holes
made before your time
I can't help but notice

how your own shoes stay empty

This Time You Save Yourself

To those who didn't receive a good morning message

To those who haven't found their passion yet or aren't sure if they will ever have one

To the ones who have never been in a relationship, on a date, or had a first kiss

To those that don't have the big friend group or collection of diplomas

To the ones who don't know if they want to have kids, settle down, or stay in the same place

Your value is entirely unchanged by arbitrary milestones.

Accepting that you may never have full
certainty is the beginning of letting go

This Time You Save Yourself

It's okay if you broke down today
it's okay if you broke down yesterday
it's okay if you've broken down
every day of this week

You're still here
and you're just as resilient and loveable as ever

This Time You Save Yourself

You should have been there

(*I needed you*)

7

This Time You Save Yourself

No one has ever
torn me apart
quite like I have
the most painful narratives
didn't come
from the mouths of others

but the stories I told myself

Emotionally-charged memories
you believed you had moved past
might still find you doubled over
in heartache at times

this doesn't mean
you haven't made progress
that you'll never get over it
or you are forever broken

You are human and letting go isn't linear.

This Time You Save Yourself

Regardless of what anyone might tell you
two things remain true:

your pain is valid
and you deserve to heal

Abandonment fear is a monster that feeds off of any innocuous sign.

Like swallowing toothpaste as a kid, it fuels itself on things that are not quite food. Squeezing the tube and convincing itself that the minty paste is sustenance. Proof that yet again, you will be abandoned. Convincing you that the sigh they just let out means they hate you, they're being silent because they don't love you anymore, their resting face is actually contorted with irritation at your existence.

While you watch this horror film play out, remember you don't have to listen to a monster struggling to survive off of scraps.

This Time You Save Yourself

There are days to come
where panic is a distant memory
swapped for serenity
where nightmares are replaced by dreams
replaced by a reality somehow better
there is lightness and ease
and it is just around the bend
of this dark corner

If you only keep moving.

This Time You Save Yourself

You are not too broken
to love and
be loved

**WARNING: PEOPLE YOU MIRROR MAY
APPEAR CLOSER THAN THEY ARE**

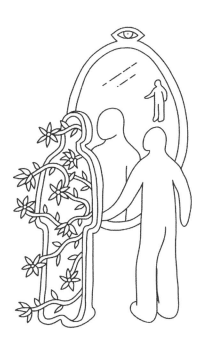

This Time You Save Yourself

People won't stop caring for you
if you get better
don't stop yourself from healing
for fear you'll lose their compassion
if you do

You don't have to be in crisis to be important.

This Time You Save Yourself

That knotted ache in your chest
is your body's way of reassuring

'I know what happened is too much
for any mind to carry
so until you're ready
I will do it for you'

This Time You Save Yourself

The most devastating love
blooms only halfway
fed by an insatiable hope
it lives in futures and maybes
a promise just out of grasp
camped on the dividing line

This Time You Save Yourself

If they put you
in a position to chase

run in the opposite direction

You shouldn't have to teach them to be a good person.

You shouldn't have to teach them how to respect others, how to be kind, to empathize and see beyond themselves. You shouldn't have to teach them not to make derogatory remarks. You shouldn't have to teach them to be patient with the barista. You shouldn't have to teach them to be considerate of unfamiliar ways of life.

You shouldn't have to teach them.

This Time You Save Yourself

You wanted them back
despite the heartache they caused
and that's nothing to be ashamed of
for you wanted love back
not them

you wanted love

At no point did you choose what happened to you.

Even if you put yourself in a position to repeat it. Even if you found yourself searching to re-live it. This was your attempt at surviving and making sense of what happened.

You are not to blame for the cruelty others chose to inflict upon you.

This Time You Save Yourself

Pain is not your enemy
it tugs at your shoulder
looking to be comforted
it wants to be noticed
befriended

I bet if you invited it in
took its prickly coat
and spent some time getting acquainted
it would soon be on its way

When you put them on a pedestal
you take away their opportunity
to show you
who they truly are

This Time You Save Yourself

You shape-shift
to please everyone else
so often you've forgotten
your original form
is worth occupying

Inside you burn, but let on next to none of your suffering. The pleasant smiles and your friendly cheer have not a hint of the night before in them. The night you spent shaking or crying or somehow worse yet - feeling nothing at all. You let your tears fall, only in the shower or when it rains so they go unnoticed.

Though I wonder if you ever consider that hiding all this pain gives it that much more life. I wonder if you know that around the right people, you don't need to keep pretending your pain doesn't exist to be acceptable.

You deserve someone
who will get you the flowers
someone who will
pick them from the garden
carefully avoiding thorns
because they might not love flowers
but they love how your face lights up
when you receive them

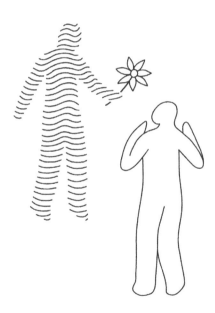

This Time You Save Yourself

You know you're going to be okay, but right now it doesn't feel like it. Right now it feels like the life you thought you knew is crumbling around you. Right now your spirit suffers a pain unimaginable to some.

Nevertheless, hear me when I say that breaking is acceptable. Aching is allowed. It's alright if you need this time to tend to the splintered shards of your heart. It's fair if all you can do is stay in bed and cry until your tears run dry.

Allow yourself time to mourn, because you know that eventually you're going to be okay, but right now you're not. How you feel in this moment, deserves to be honoured.

This Time You Save Yourself

You loved everyone else
just a little too much
until there was none left
for you

This Time You Save Yourself

Just because it didn't work out
doesn't mean they don't miss you

they look for you in melodies
and inside jokes
their head still turns
when they hear a laugh
with the ring of your voice in it
or catch your perfume
on a passing stranger
they notice the empty spaces
where your things
used to take their place

Just because you're not there
doesn't mean your absence isn't felt.

This Time You Save Yourself

Their lack of effort
does not mean
you should take it
upon yourself
to put in more

I know it's been a while and you thought you were over it, but it's all coming up now because you're finally ready to face the last of this pain. On the surface it appears to be a step backwards, but sage minds know better than to believe appearances. This is a clear sign that you are safe and secure enough now to wave a white flag at this torment. That you have done the work to get to this place where the deeper cutting hurt is available for reconcile.

As a dandelion gone to seed, you are ready to release, to allow segments of your suffering to float off on the wind leaving room to start anew.

How many hearts
did you have to burn through
to learn how to stoke a fire
in your own?

This Time You Save Yourself

You cannot keep falling for people
who rip open your wounds

your unhealed injuries
deserve to be tended to
by someone who wraps them
in understanding
secured with delicate sensitivity
and emotional safety

This Time You Save Yourself

They pick you up
and put you down
just to get to where they want
you fall between the cracks
found only to be forgotten again

bite back this time
for you are no one's plaything

Your human need
for love
is not

'*needy*'

You may not be as shy as you believe, you may have simply been around people who don't accept you for far too long.

Perhaps you would be a fuller version of yourself if you weren't having to worry about being judged. Perhaps if you search for spaces where your voice is listened to and valued

you would use it more.

This Time You Save Yourself

A love awaits
to embrace you wholly as you are
without pretending
or changing any little bit of you

A love awaits
that won't leave you in tears at night
won't leave you begging
for scraps of affection
that will do everything in its power
not to hurt you

A love awaits
to restore your faith
and smooth your jagged edges

A love awaits to welcome you
without the promise of injury
you've grown accustom to

This Time You Save Yourself

You are too precious
to be crossing oceans
for someone who refuses
to make the journey

from their couch to the door

This Time You Save Yourself

It's a unique kind of ache

to grieve someone
still very much alive

to grieve a relationship
you never really had

to grieve an absence
never before filled

it wounds and swells
as injuries do
but leaves marks concealed

Translations you must know:

Sometimes '*needy*' means
'I'm only interested in getting my own needs
met, so any of yours are an inconvenience'

Sometimes '*sensitive*' means
'You're in touch with feelings that I have been
actively trying to repress. Instead of coming to
terms with my own, it's easier to shame you for
yours'

Sometimes '*too much*' means
'Your acceptance of yourself and confidence to
voice your needs makes me feel inadequate and
insecure'

Sometimes '*closed off*' means
'I don't like that you have a life beyond me and
won't sacrifice your privacy for my comfort'

This Time You Save Yourself

Sadness does not last forever
eventually you fill
the empty chasms
with so much joy
there is no space left
for the sorrow to cling

This Time You Save Yourself

Loveable from the moment
you came to be
how tragic it was
to be surrounded
by those who made you feel

you had to earn your birthright

This Time You Save Yourself

It's not easy, is it?
fighting a perpetual battle in your mind
thrown into a war
you never enlisted for
forced to make weapons of your mistrust

but circumstances are different now
peace is within arms reach
the last battle is just you against yourself
and maybe it doesn't have to be a violent one

This Time You Save Yourself

You don't have to break
your own heart
for fear that if you don't
do it yourself
someone else might

Sometimes I fear I am living on the sidelines. That I am peering through the window of someone's home to catch them in an intimate moment - sitting down together for a meal shared in good company. I have always felt alone, no matter who was around or how loudly they cheered for me. I cry on my birthday every year as if it were tradition and I don't think I could fill a room full of people if I tried.

Perhaps there is comfort in that. Even if I am the only one in this room, *I am here wherever I go and that can never be taken away*. Perhaps there is comfort in knowing that most of us feel this way occasionally and even in loneliness we are connected. If someone looked through my window I think they'd see me gradually becoming content with solitude.

This Time You Save Yourself

I trim my hair to cut the memories it holds
discarding them like split ends
they run from the very base
cracking at every new inch that seems to grow

Late at night
I pull apart my segments
like oranges on the tree
outside my window

I wonder if they feel the pain
of cracking open as well

This Time You Save Yourself

Liminal spaces:

airports
parking lots at night
waiting rooms
empty tunnels and hallways

Spaces that should not be liminal:

the conditions of their love for you

This Time You Save Yourself

You deserve a love
that doesn't
hurt your heart
to wake up to

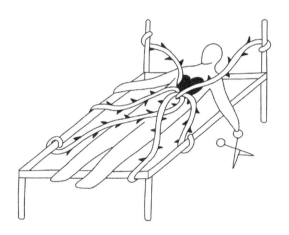

This Time You Save Yourself

They said you were too weak
too fragile
too sensitive
not because you are defective
but because they lacked the wisdom
to see the strength in your tenderness

This Time You Save Yourself

I hope you ask for more
I hope you tell them what you want
I hope your standards are not so easily met
I hope you make your boundaries clear
I hope you don't swallow your thoughts
I hope you are inconvenient
I hope you don't settle for less
I hope access to you requires kind-heartedness,
dedication, effort and consistency

You always deserved to take up space
in love's hands.

This Time You Save Yourself

Don't ignore red flags
for the sake of not being alone

This Time You Save Yourself

You shouldn't have to bury
the bar underground
to save yourself
from being disappointed

I won't pick myself apart to see
if you love me or

love

me

not

This Time You Save Yourself

How I wish you understood
you were never a burden
to be endured
suffered
or tolerated

This Time You Save Yourself

When they label you strong
you find yourself recoiling

maybe you don't want to be strong
perhaps you want to be soft
taken care of
treated well
and loved
you want peace and ease
and lack of any need to be *'strong'*

This Time You Save Yourself

I cannot turn off the tap of my love
I can wrench and screw the handle
until it appears tightly sealed
but it will still drip

abandoning love is futile
so I must learn who is worth
turning the tap for

This Time You Save Yourself

I fit into this world best
at my sickest
people praised me
for disappearing
the less of me there was
the more acceptable I became

I no longer care to fit into this world.

This Time You Save Yourself

There is a love out there
that will gently nurture
the glow in your chest
instead of setting it alight
and letting it burn you to ashes

This Time You Save Yourself

You may have lost them
but don't forget
they lost you too

they lost the depth you breathe into life
the way you turn stale moments into art

you may have lost them

but
          they
                    lost
                              you
                                        too

This Time You Save Yourself

You only love like that once

You're never as reckless twice

This Time You Save Yourself

The sun glimmers
a nebulous flare
though I know one day it will rain again
in fact one day it will storm heavily
but with this knowledge
I cherish its euphoric presence
knowing that it will return
time and time again

So too must I savour happiness
when it calls
for it may pass
but it too will return

This Time You Save Yourself

They couldn't give you what you needed
they made you a bed of thorns
and you pricked yourself every night
pretending theirs was a healing love
as you gradually bled out

This Time You Save Yourself

The suffering was not silent
it wasn't brooding or mysterious
tinged with manic-pixie romanticism

The suffering was loud and constant
it was all white and flashing lights
it was *'hear me'* in an empty room

This Time You Save Yourself

I will not keep cleaning
the gory messes of others
to the detriment
of myself

This Time You Save Yourself

If their love has gone stale
like day old coffee
if commitment has soured
and effort gone cold
I hope you stop returning
for another bitter sip

This Time You Save Yourself

They said
it never meant anything
as if that changed
what it meant
to you

This Time You Save Yourself

Your childhood self leapt fearlessly
with the assurance
that bruises always fade
gashes mend
and bones fuse whole

When did you lose confidence
in your ability to heal?

This Time You Save Yourself

They licked your wounds
like the hero
pretending they weren't responsible
for inflicting them

They chose to do to you
what you could have never done to them

And that is the difference.

This Time You Save Yourself

You are not tainted
by the things
that have happened to you

scars don't take away
from your purity

innocence is a gift
you get to keep
forever

This Time You Save Yourself

I hide pieces of myself
within you
like forgotten earrings

I just want an excuse to keep coming back.

You're going to make mistakes.

In the excitement of being wanted, you'll be seduced into choosing the wrong person. You'll agree to things your spirit does not. You'll hurt the ones you love and let people down. You might even let yourself down a few times. You're going to make these mistakes because you're exploring the world, yourself and this ever-in-flux dynamic. When you do, know that you are learning. Every time you gain a little more clarity on what you do and don't want. What you will and won't accept. Who you do and don't want to be.

You are endlessly discovering yourself and that requires making mistakes along the way.

I crumbled to the ground
trying to build us
a solid foundation
with just
a single
pair of
hands

This Time You Save Yourself

There are many drugs
one can try
just a few times
without developing
an addiction

You are not one of them.

This Time You Save Yourself

If you live in your hurt
you cannot be disappointed
if you turn off the light within
there is no way to cast a shadow

but a life lived in darkness
is eternally void of colour
and with the risk of opening yourself
comes the potential for auroras

This Time You Save Yourself

Your soul feels less yellow today
and that is okay

like the yellow of butter on toast
you melt
disillusioned with it all
blending into the old
forgotten jasmine tea
sitting beside your bed

today you are drained of all yellow
wind whipped hair
buttercup reflections
somersaults
today you cannot and do not need
to save anyone but yourself

This Time You Save Yourself

I don't have any second chances left
I gave one too many
to someone
who used them up
for everyone to come

You are the expert on yourself
no one has the right to tell you
what your needs are
which ones are valid
how to feel
or what to do

You don't get a chance to develop better
judgment if you're not allowed to practice your
own.

This Time You Save Yourself

You must stop diving
in front of bullets
when the one
who claims to love you
is the same person
pulling the trigger

And while you can help me
rearrange my broken pieces
I cannot expect you
to act as glue

This Time You Save Yourself

You have spent far too long despising your body, the vessel that allows you to experience all this life has to offer.

Obsolete are the days of pinching and sucking in. Tilting your head in the mirror to see if you look more appealing at a different angle. It's time to entomb the restrictive punishments and over-exertion.

This body is your channel between all that you encompass and the beauty of the natural world. Your relationship with it may change day to day, but like any other living being, it is worthy of your respect. It deserves the same hospitality you grant everyone else.

This Time You Save Yourself

It poisons you from inside out
the bitterness, that is,
it masquerades as a safety net
while tangling around you
tighter and tighter
until it strangles every last drop
of vulnerability

the precursor to unconditional love

You were borne of thunder and chaos. Raised
under ever-shifting conditions. Your only
certainty in knowing that things will always
change. Now constancy has the touch of alien. A
newcomer you had regularly imagined
welcoming, yet her handshake feels
unexpectedly threatening.

She is new. She is wrapped in balance, and when
you take her jacket for the night, you reveal an
ensemble of monotony and boredom. You fail to
see that the fabric is made of trustworthiness, for
you've never felt it before.

This Time You Save Yourself

You have spent too much time
justifying their actions
to the jury in your mind
that knows you deserve better

This Time You Save Yourself

I'm sure I heard
the moment
my heart hit the floor
it sounded like absence
it sounded like disappointment
it sounded like disapproval
as cold as your shoulder
the one I used to lay my head on

This Time You Save Yourself

They wanted you
in the way that people want fake plants
they wanted you
but without the management

you only come in one edition
and it requires wanting all of you

This Time You Save Yourself

When you're ready
you will take that magnifying glass
you use to analyse your flaws
and search for all the goodness
in yourself instead

This Time You Save Yourself

It doesn't end like this
sobbing on the floor
cheek pressed against the cold hardness
of wood and the world
this chapter of wounds ends here

but your story continues

Re-building

This Time You Save Yourself

You left me a husk of myself
so I rebuilt
remodelled
I renovated
from the ground up
I got to know every little detail
and in the process

I fell in love with my creation

This Time You Save Yourself

There comes a time
where your heart
no longer drops into your stomach
when you hear their name

where memories of them
no longer corrode at your serenity
and the anniversary
of their departure
passes without a thought

This Time You Save Yourself

My love outgrew yours
but the growing pains taught me
how to tend to myself first

This Time You Save Yourself

You have made a home of your trauma
a familiar nest
safe in its predictable unpredictability

but now it is time for you to move out
to assemble something new
borne of your healing

This Time You Save Yourself

Your heart knows when it is time to release
slowly it lays memories to rest
the timbre of their voice
the spice of their perfume
what their hand felt like in yours
and while feelings remain
your heart strides forward

one day you will catch up to it

You can grow
beyond the things
that have happened to you

This Time You Save Yourself

Held down by the weight
of bricks on your chest
you're pressed like a flower
drying

underneath you retain
your colour and delicacy
preserved ever-longer

waiting to return again

"Where do I belong
if not in your arms"

The child within you begs

The way people walk speaks volumes.

Some will walk ahead of you, far off in the distance. Never turning to notice you're miles apart.

Some will make a point of walking beside you. Adjusting their speed to match yours, regardless of their own capacity.

I believe a person's capacity for patience lies in the way they walk, and I can only hope you find someone who chooses to walk next to you.

Something good is on its way

Be here for it.

Wait for someone who is committed to learning about you.

Wait for someone who is curious and genuinely interested in understanding the highlights and shadows of the world through your lens. Look for someone who will not only listen to your struggles and pitfalls, but go out of their way to read and educate themselves on how they can best support you.

Find someone who won't stop after finding out your favourite food, but who will take the time to learn the recipe. Wait for someone who pays attention to how your past effects your present. Wait for someone who will learn more about themselves, in order to keep you from unintentional harm.

Wait for someone who is dedicated to continually learning about you as a changing being.

This Time You Save Yourself

You have an incredible ability to repair
your body works at putting itself
back together relentlessly

bone

tissue

and yes

your trust in yourself as well

I know you gave up on love, because it split you in two and somehow left you with neither side of yourself. Nothing but bitterness intact. I know you've made a pact not to repeat the same mistakes - that of believing in something so dangerously ruinous.

But the truth is your injured heart gradually fuses back together. Eventually you stop looking at couples with disdain, envisioning yourself in their place again.

Sooner or later you take a wild chance, even if your head screams at you not to, but this time it doesn't split you in two. This time it helps you adhere the sparse bits of hope back together.

This Time You Save Yourself

I assembled a fortress around myself
at the cost of my softness
I decided watching myself disappear
behind a wall
was worse than opening myself
to an unpredictable world

At least in this one there's the possibility
of a good and safe hand to hold

This is for you:

The one who is always giving more than they get back

The one who is there for everyone else even when no one is there for you

This is for you and your tireless generosity that would kill for just an ounce of what you give to everyone else

This is for you, a reminder to give at least a few of those ounces to yourself

This Time You Save Yourself

What if
instead of being so hard on yourself
you tried being gentle instead?

You are not over the top or high maintenance for having boundaries.

No matter how normalised something is, you are allowed to honour your discomfort. Others may judge them, but they are yours for a reason. Whether it makes sense or not to anyone else does not change their validity.

You're allowed to draw lines in the sand within which you can still feel safe and comfortable. You're allowed to distance yourself from those who cannot respect those lines or try to alter them.

This Time You Save Yourself

If today you felt any of the following:

> paranoia, jealousy, anger, depression, grief, yearning, hopelessness or unlovableness

Remember that while you were feeling these, you were still:

> beautiful, valuable, important, intelligent, warm-hearted and full of light

Having bad feelings does not make you a bad person.

This Time You Save Yourself

If you choose to live inside your head
I hope you decide to make it a beautiful scene
I hope you patiently decorate it
with admiration and self-compassion
showing grace to the crevices
yet to be cleaned of their cobwebs

I hope you learn to live
amongst those cobwebs
with the empathy they require
and the freedom to leave
strand
by
strand

This Time You Save Yourself

They planted a seed of doubt
watered and watched tendrils of self-hatred
grow around you like vines

Their power thrived only when yours wilted.

This Time You Save Yourself

Things that don't make you *'weak'*:

> expressing sadness
> expressing your needs
> being sensitive
> feeling anxious
> needing rest
> stopping at or before your limits

This Time You Save Yourself

Every reason
you find to continue
leads you to another

and one day,
all of a sudden,
existing stops
feeling like warfare

This Time You Save Yourself

You have to start assuming the best for yourself. You have to start assuming that people like you. You have to start assuming they care about you. You have to start assuming that no one is mad at you, that you are a good person and that people enjoy your company. I know it's hard when the opposite message is engrained in your way of being, but you have to start contesting it.

You're worth the peace that comes with assuming the best.

Life is too short to be motivated by anything other than love.

Treat people with as much kindness and compassion as you can muster (an exceedingly difficult task and one that requires lots of practice). Do your best and know that what that might entail is allowed to fluctuate day-to-day. Make an effort. Really truly make as much of an effort as you can. Tell people you love them whenever you get the chance. If you've been blessed with enough energy, try to be present for life and don't take it for granted. The earth will one day hold you the way the people who care for you do, so for now embrace them when you can.

Someone somewhere out there is feeling exactly
what you are right now

Isn't that staggeringly beautiful?
you know nothing of each other
and yet you are connected in this moment
by an emotion
a humanness

This Time You Save Yourself

A love letter to my inner child:

you are full of starlight and wonder
you see what others do not
hear what is unsaid
you sense a magic easily unnoticed

I will always be a welcome host
to your curiosity
your playfulness
and your unadulterated delight

You won't always hide from who you are.

Your passion will be ignited again for the music that made your younger heart race. You will sing in the shower and hunt out childhood favourite foods just for fun, the kind with sprinkles or the flavour of bubblegum.

However this time, you'll embrace it. This time you'll accept yourself. You will glow again for all of the shamed parts you dimmed and draw people who adore that your eyes still glitter when you think of collecting blackberries in your lunchbox and searching for a face in the moon.

You play a game of hide and seek
with past versions of yourself
that went missing

You can radically decide that you like your life
even if you see improvements for it
even if you are not yet fully satisfied

You can decide now that the life you've built
is a good one that can be expanded upon
rather than a subpar one that must be fixed

This Time You Save Yourself

Release yourself from the burden
of having to convince anyone
to care for you

release your commitment
to those who refuse
to commit you to memory

When you want or have to start over it's natural to feel hesitant about beginning late. The pressure of needing to rebuild everything quickly for fear of running behind is a trick. There is always time to start fresh on your own timeline.

You don't have to 'catch up' to anyone else for your pursuit to be worthwhile.

This Time You Save Yourself

When they come back
think twice
before you
open the door

You are still loveable.

On your bad days and good. When you're mad, anxious, jealous or overcome with any other ungainly emotion. You're still loveable when your body changes and your clothes fit differently. When they leave or when someone new comes along. When you make mistakes and when you don't get the job, the acceptance letter or the outcome you hoped for. You're still loveable when you don't reach unattainable standards and when you give up on trying to. You're still loveable when you don't think you are. Even now, reading this and feeling somehow that you must be the exception, you are still loveable.

This Time You Save Yourself

You loved them
for all the beautiful parts of yourself
you could not see
so you projected those parts
onto the canvas in front of you instead

You were not preprogrammed to believe everyone you love will leave you, or that you're never good enough. That no one really enjoys your company or that you have to achieve perfection to be worthy.

At some point you inherited these beliefs from those around you. However, just as you were forced to learn these connections, you have the power and adaptability to unlearn them as well. You are capable of choosing compassion in their place.

This Time You Save Yourself

And that is the beauty
of bearing a heart like yours
its depth is worth every scar
collected along its quest

You planned a whole future with a person you once believed to be 'the one'. Never did you imagine there would come a time where you no longer speak to each other. You swore they were your last love.

Meanwhile, your future self is singing in the car with their favourite person, racing each other down the hallway and picking herbs from the garden for a dinner planned together.

You don't see it now, but love is not limited to just one person.

This Time You Save Yourself

They liked the way
you looked in their life
but you are more
than decor

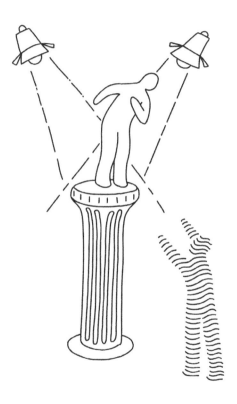

It's actually very much worth your time to go after what you're dreaming of. Regardless of how 'unrealistic' it may seem in anyone's eyes, including your own. You might succeed. If you don't, it might lead you to a new passion. If it doesn't, you might find you grow from the experience of going after it.

You have something to gain from dreaming, irrespective of whether it's followed by success.

This Time You Save Yourself

Refuse to accept love
solely given as a reward

- *conditional*

As a function of being human, you are inherently deserving. I'm sorry that you've been convinced otherwise. I'm sorry that you feel compelled to perform and grovel in the hope of reaching a threshold of 'enoughness', as if you weren't intrinsically enough just by being here.

There is nothing about you that needs to be changed to deserve to be treated with care, patience, empathy and compassion. There is nothing you could do to nullify this fundamental right.

Until your very last breath, *you will always be deserving.*

This Time You Save Yourself

First you survive the suffering
then you transform it
into something monumental

you pan for gold in your pain
with a pen
a paintbrush
your actions
or your voice

This Time You Save Yourself

In the palm of your hand
I place my trust
praying you never
ball your fists

This Time You Save Yourself

The world looks safer
painted black and white

the most fearless thing you can do
is to exist within the grey

A day of rest is never a wasted day.

Just because you didn't do anything productive by society's standards, does not mean you have thrown a day away. A day of rest is good for your health - mental and physical. A day of rest is good for inspiring creativity and motivation. There's a lot to be gained from doing very little.

This Time You Save Yourself

You've always been skilled
at turning dirt into gold
so when they ask you
why you stayed
therein lies your answer

This Time You Save Yourself

The sun glistens
and you're alive
people embrace at airports and train stations
and you're alive
the coffee you curl your fingers around
warms your wintery palms
and you're alive
you are loved and lucky
and life is full of surprises
and like it or not

You are alive.

Your greatest fears
are nothing
in the
face of
you

This Time You Save Yourself

Soft as overripe fruit
bruised like a peach
and yet you still have the courage to care
brave enough to offer yourself on a platter
for the potential at easing
someone else's suffering
this is not martyrdom
nor naivety to the ruthlessness of it all
this is grit and spirit
this is humankind
at its kindest

This Time You Save Yourself

You became a star
watching over
twinkling with affection
and while I could not always see you
on clouded nights
or through silky blue skies
you were always there

You are always here with me.

You can spend lots of time learning and growing
and still not know the answers.

You are not obligated to find the solutions to
every problem. It doesn't make you any less
wise or healed. You don't need to have every
explanation, every remedy or response.

But on days where everyone else has failed me
Under heavy hands that crush rather than hold
Between you and me

*I am just happy to come home and make pasta sauce
with you.*

The coping mechanisms you're outgrowing:

avoiding, ignoring, staying passive, hiding,
shirking responsibility, blaming and tearing
yourself down

The coping mechanisms growing in their place:

accepting, feeling, actively searching, listening
to your inner dialogue, awareness,
communicating your needs, respecting your
agency and owning your actions

You will live many different lives. Not solely in a spiritual sense, but in the way that you will change your hair and move to new places. You might find yourself amidst people with entirely different interests or wake up along an unexpected career path with renewed purpose. You will discover new, exciting little passions that lie dormant inside until you go in search of them. Your lifestyle will shift and priorities will change many times over. You will live a myriad of lives and each will shape and polish you into a novel and thrilling version of yourself.

Strength
is being kinder
than the way
you've been treated

This Time You Save Yourself

Someday it will dawn on you
that the life you are living
is the reality you once dreamed of

you will live in a home
where peace is expected
you will forget to suck in your stomach
and love will be a guarantee not a question

As small and insignificant as you may feel
remember you are a living
breathing
piece of the universe
a part of something greater

You are proof that there is kindness in this world. That there are people who go out of their way to show they care. You are proof that deep, lasting, unconditional love exists. You are proof that there is always someone willing to listen, to be there, to lend a helping hand. If you struggle to find it around you, you only have to look inside to be reminded that humanity always triumphs.

This Time You Save Yourself

I want a lazy love
a love that naps
a love that can be in the same room
without talking
a low-energy love
I want a love with a hand
that finds its way to mine subconsciously
a love that requires little explaining
I want a love that knows
not because I told it so
but because it simply understands

This Time You Save Yourself

One day someone will see you
beyond the way you see yourself

Hearts are not meant to be restrained and untouched. Hearts are made for opening, breaking and cementing back together again. Hearts are made for growing and collecting holes of experience along the way. Hearts are made to be used, to pump love through your veins.

If your heart is scarred and sensitive in a few places, I hope you see that for what it is.

A testament to your courage to love.

This Time You Save Yourself

You are good enough
at every age
size
and stage of life

There is so much more to embrace beyond romantic love. There's the love you feel for your best friend, platonic and lastin. For your family - blood or chosen. Affection you can only share between a beloved pet. The enthusiasm that courses through your veins for your passions. Most importantly, there's the enlightening types of love you feel for yourself - growing and curious.

I hope you never limit your experience of love, for there is far more to explore than merely the romantic kind.

This Time You Save Yourself

No more atmospheric highs
and tunneling lows
I wish for the stability
of a firmly rooted oak
placid
settled
and ever-growing towards the light

You need two types of people in your life.

The first type will swim the depths with you.
They will turn their flashlight on ready to
explore the darkness. These are the people who
spin time into an afterthought, lost in
introspective reflection and relatable stories.

The second type will wade in the shallow end.
They will help you come up for air every now
and then. They possess a magical ability for
spirited laughter. They are joie-de-vivre
embodied.

You need two types of people and if you find
both in one you must never let go.

This Time You Save Yourself

Because there is no one after you
and really there was no one before you
not really
not in a way that ever mattered

This Time You Save Yourself

When love comes knocking at your door
I hope you let it in
I hope you pull up a chair and give it a chance
I hope you accept all of it
without checking once, twice, three times
for a knife behind its back

when love pulls you in for an embrace
I hope this time you take a step forwards

This Time You Save Yourself

You became so light
so very full of light
you wanted to illuminate
every dark corner of yourself

You had been afraid of your own darkness for too long

This Time You Save Yourself

Within you is an undiscovered goldmine
within you is everything you crave
unwavering support and
steadfast belief in yourself
a cocoon of safety
and springs of hope

You only have to look inside
for all you've ever wanted

Understanding is a bandaid
that repairs
even the most
fragmented heart

This Time You Save Yourself

Tell them you love them
tell them every chance you get
spread it thick like jam
express it freely

because 'I love you' is not a scarce resource
it doesn't have to be used sparingly
to have meaning

This Time You Save Yourself

You do not have to pretend or perform for me
I see you as you are
and I love you just the same
even without the smile you plaster
for everyone else to see
I am here with you
when hope is too slippery for you to grasp

it's okay

here -

borrow some of mine

This Time You Save Yourself

How lucky to be on this rock at the same time
walking hand-in-hand
spending our days
fighting for the last bit of leftovers
and finding your socks
mixed in with mine

I sit with her. That little girl whose hair was yanked and pulled hastily into place. I comb it with care, letting it fall where it pleases. I whisper kindness into her until the 'you're not enough and somehow also too much' is rustled out of her bones. I spoon-feed her patience as I lovingly watch her stumble through adolescence and crash into adulthood. Learning lessons she might not have had to if she were handled by more delicate hands. I do not scold her when she breaks a vase, and she breaks *many* of them. She calls for me and I come ready to listen and understand. Ready to love her as she is.

I have learnt to love her as she is. Grapefruit juice dripping down her forearms. Shards of cracked porcelain at her feet.

This Time You Save Yourself

When they become
part of your routine
and your perfumes
start to blend together
you must never forget
the scent of your own

This Time You Save Yourself

You're allowed to be all contradictions

longing to settle down
while your feet itch to roam
bouncing with excitement
and basking in inactivity
quietly humble
and glittering with pride

There are hundreds of versions of you
and you're allowed to be them at once
endlessly traversing their extremities

And while the universe
may or may not
be full of magic

you certainly are

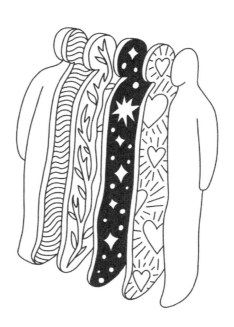

This Time You Save Yourself

The tradition of passing trauma
from generation to generation
like a family heirloom
stops with you
its final inheritor
determined to lay it to rest

This time…

> you wrap your arms around yourself
> when you begin to feel the cracks

This time…

> you use grace as sealant, in place of
> berating yourself

This time…

> you're reminded of the storms you've
> outlasted and you're sure of your
> permanence despite the monsoons

This time you save yourself.

Dearest reader,

If you have made it this far I would like to take a moment to express my gratitude to you.

Please consider leaving a review on Amazon or Goodreads. Not only does this help to reach new hearts in search of healing, but it is also a welcome gift to receive your feedback and hear your own story.

MORE FROM ZARA BAS

I Have to Tell You Something (2022)

Soft and hard truths written from the most tender depths of a healing heart, these are the words your inner child needs to hear

Take What You Need (2023)

Essays and aphorisms that break down the journey to peace and provide a roadmap to get there

ACKNOWLEDGMENTS

The process of assembling a book requires not one, but a number of souls. Behind these pages lies the support of a village.

Thank you to my supportive father, the first to teach me to read and write via Grover's embarrassment. Thank you to my ever-curious mother who inspires me to search for magic in every living being, spores and all. Thank you to my generous brother, who always gave extra of his portion of Shapes and to my go-getter sister, who is still teaching me the art of sharing (I'm sure we must still have each other's clothes).

Thank you to my twinkling stars, one who answers my texts at 1am and the other who nurtured my love for wielding words through bribes of Jubes during long car rides.

Thank you to Mimi for nurturing my love for creative pursuits with her seemingly endless knowledge, her library fit for the state and all-too-big collection of crafting materials.

Thank you to my best friend, Nat, whose tea time chats brighten my days (even if only through the phone) and hugs I could not live without. Thank you to Niks, who has requested that I make it known that he is my biggest fan, and to Iz - a constant source of spiritual inspiration.

Thank you to the incredibly talented, PinnochiJo for bringing the words in this book to life through illustration. I am still pinching myself at the opportunity to collaborate with an artist I once dreamed of working with.

Thank you to Shushu and Ayi, whose delicious home-cooked meals are as warm as their hearts (感谢叔叔阿姨，他们的美味家常菜，正如他们的心一样温暖。).

Finally, to my partner who has offered me more patience, love and laughs than I knew existed, thank you for teaching me that life is sweeter as a team.

Printed in Great Britain
by Amazon